D0766625

JOBS

First published 2013 by
A & C Black, an imprint of Bloomsbury Publishing Plc
50 Bedford Square, London, WC1B 3DP

www.bloomsbury.com

ISBN 978-1-4081-8172-0

Printed and bound by CPI Group (UK) Ltd, Croydon CR0 4YY

1 3 5 7 9 10 8 6 4 2

World's WORST JOBS

TRACEY TURNER

Illustrated by Garry Davies

A & C BLACK
AN IMPRINT OF BLOOMSBURY
LONDON NEW DELHI NEW YORK SYDNEY

CONTENTS

Dangerous Jobs

Disgusting Jobs

Poisonous Jobs

Gory Jobs

Horrible Jobs

How to Avoid the World's Worst Jobs

KEY TO SALARY:

£ = Almost nothing

££ = Not a lot

£££ = A living wage

££££ = Nice little earner

£££££ = Rolling in money

DANGEROUS JOBS

From the Stone Age to the present day, people have earned a living doing a wide variety of hazardous jobs. Perils include steep cliffs, enormous falling trees, deadly diseases and fights to the death...

LUMBERJACK

WANTED:
Lumberjack

DUTIES: Cutting down trees, hauling them out of the forest, and getting them ready for transport.

SALARY: ££

KEY SKILLS AND ATTRIBUTES:
- Fitness, strength and general toughness are essential.
- Ability to operate dangerous machinery an advantage, though training can be given.
- Only tough, outdoorsy-types need apply.
- Must enjoy time in the wilderness and the company of other lumberjacks.

Ah, the life of a simple lumberjack: striding manfully through the forest, at one with nature, the fresh air scented with pine resin and ringing with the sound of chainsaws . . . you might be wondering how this can be one of the world's worst jobs?

Timber!

A lumberjack's job is one of the most dangerous in the world. Although there's plenty of healthy fresh air to breathe, there are also plenty of hazards. Lumberjacks use chainsaws to cut down trees – and chainsaws have also been known to cut bits off the people operating them, often with fatal results. In the days before chainsaws, swinging sharp axes around could be hazardous too.

But the most dangerous part of a lumberjack's job is the enormous, heavy falling trees. (After all, this is the whole point of the job.) To cut down a tree, lumberjacks cut a wedge in one side – this is the way they want the tree to fall. Then they saw through the other side. The tree should fall in the direction of the wedge, but it doesn't always. Since trees can be very tall and very heavy, there's a risk of being squashed that's impossible to ignore.

Putting cables around felled trees to transport them can be dangerous too – the steel cables can snap under extreme tension, acting as giant metal whips that can cause severe injuries. To make things worse, lumberjacks' jobs tend to be in remote areas, which means that they're a long way from the nearest hospital if there's an accident.

Safety First

In the old days, safety equipment consisted of a pair of stout boots and a bandage if you accidentally hacked your arm off with an axe. Nowadays, lumberjacks wear hard hats, steel-capped boots and Kevlar trousers to protect them, and ear protectors to save them from the deafening noise of chainsaws. Even so, it's a perilous occupation – and one that doesn't always pay very well to make up for it.

ANCIENT ROMAN GLADIATOR

WANTED: Gladiator

DUTIES: Fighting and/or dying (in the most entertaining way possible).

SALARY: Board and lodging at gladiator school.

KEY SKILLS AND ATTRIBUTES:
- Must be strong, muscly and as tough as a legionary's old boots.
- Some sword skills an advantage, though full training will be given.
- Fearlessness in the face of certain death and pitiless cruelty are both strong advantages.
- Would suit slave and/or criminal.

The gladiators who fought in the ancient Roman games certainly had a dangerous job. They ended up having to fight other gladiators in front of screaming, bloodthirsty crowds — sometimes to the death!

Gruesome Games

All over the Roman Empire, games were held as entertainment for the people – ordinary folk and VIPs alike. They were a bit like modern football games . . . except a lot more gruesome. The Roman games were held in huge, oval-shaped arenas seating hundreds if not thousands of spectators. The entertainment often began with a procession of all the people who were going to take part. Then there might be animal fights; maybe a few prisoners thrown to the lions, a wrestling match, a mock battle for the army to show off its skills, and perhaps a nice public execution to keep the crowds happy.

But the gladiator fighting was the highlight.

Slaves, Prisoners, Volunteers and an Emperor or Two

Most gladiators were slaves or prisoners. They didn't have much choice about what they did for a living, and were the property of the gladiator school owner. Sometimes, strange though it might seem, free men (and women) volunteered to fight as gladiators.

There were even emperors who fought as gladiators in public: Emperor Caligula, who was famous for being cruel and mad, and Emperor Commodus, who was pretty similar, both fought in the arena. Commodus cheated by giving his opponents useless weapons, so he always won.

Fighting School

So that they put on a good show, gladiators were specially trained in gladiator schools and became strong, fit and skilled fighters. They needed to be excellent fighters to please the crowds – if they were entertaining to watch they'd be highly valued – which meant they were a lot less likely to die in the arena.

Murmillo or Hoplomachus

There were different types of gladiator to make things more interesting for the audience. A Sagittarius fought with a bow and arrow; and a Retiarius fought with a net and trident (a kind of three pronged spear). Some gladiators were armed to represent the soldiers of a particular nationality: for example a Hoplomachus had the spear and short sword of a Greek warrior, while a Murmillo looked more like a Roman soldier, though with a helmet shaped like a fish! There were popular pairings for fights too – a Hoplomachus and a Murmillo were often pitted against one another.

Girl Gladiators

Women could be gladiators too, though it wasn't common. Because they were rare, they'd probably draw a big crowd. Two women gladiators are shown in a marble carving found in the ancient city of Halicarnassus (modern-day Bodrum in Turkey).

14

They're carrying swords and shields and wear protection on their arms and legs, but they don't have helmets on, perhaps so that the crowd can see that they're women more clearly. Emperor Severus banned women gladiators in AD 200 – maybe it was too shocking, even for the ancient Romans – but the ban didn't last for long!

Gladiator Superstars

A really successful gladiator could become famous. He (or she) would also be far less likely to die in the arena (after all, you wouldn't want to kill off the star of the show) and probably wouldn't have to fight as often.

Eventually, a really successful gladiator might earn his or her freedom. Occasionally, freedom might be awarded to a gladiator who showed extreme courage or skill during a contest.

For more on ancient Roman slavery, see page 103.

RAT CATCHER

WANTED: Rat Catcher

DUTIES: Catching and extermination of rats.

SALARY: ££

KEY SKILLS AND ATTRIBUTES:
- Must have quick reflexes and a robust immune system.
- Own terriers and ferrets a strong advantage.
- Must enjoy working alone.
- Squeamish individuals need not apply.

Rats spread disease, they'll eat almost anything, and they bite. If you're reading this in a big city, the chances are you're not far from a rat right now. No wonder rat catchers have always been in demand.

Dogs and Ferrets

Today's rat catchers use traps and poisoned bait, just as they have for hundreds of years. It's a pretty gruesome job – collecting dead rats from traps probably isn't on most people's career wish-list. But things were even worse, and a lot riskier, in the past.

People who got rid of rats would turn up at a rat-infested building with a terrier dog as well as traps, and perhaps some ferrets for good measure, making the whole business incredibly gory. The rat catcher would block up all the rat holes he could find, except one. Then he'd let his rat-catching animals loose and wait for the escaping rats to come belting out of the one remaining hole.

Often the rat catcher would pull them out with his bare hands. Since rats, especially frightened ones, often bite, and because they carry all sorts of nasty diseases, this was a highly dangerous job. Diseases spread by rats include leptospirosis (also known as Weil's disease), rat-bite fever, salmonella and plague – all of which can be fatal.

Rat Fights

Not all of the rats that rat catchers caught were killed.
Read no further if you're squeamish, because the
reason for keeping the rats was utterly revolting: rat
fighting (known as rat baiting) used to be a horrible
form of entertainment until around the beginning of
the twentieth century.

Rat baiting usually happened in pubs. The rats would
be let loose in a round pit dug into the floor, then a dog
would be released to try and kill them. People would
bet on how many rats each dog could kill. Rat baiting
became especially popular after laws were passed
making it illegal to bait bigger animals, such as bears.
Although this was terrible news for the animals, it was
great news for the rat catcher, who was well paid for
the rats he supplied.

EGG COLLECTOR

WANTED: Egg Collector

DUTIES: Abseiling down cliff faces to collect seabird eggs.

SALARY: If you're lucky, some eggs.

KEY SKILLS AND ATTRIBUTES:
- Candidates must be fairly small and light, with a head for heights.
- Must enjoy standing on tiny ledges while shooing away flocks of squawking birds.
- A steady hand is essential.
- Candidates with vertigo or a fear of birds need not apply.

Collecting seabirds' eggs from almost vertical cliff faces, with very little safety equipment, has gone on for thousands of years, and in some parts of the world it still continues today.

Going to Eggstremes

In the Arctic Circle the land is too hard and frozen to grow crops. People have to rely on animals for food, and even though getting them is incredibly dangerous, guillemots' eggs are such a good source of protein that they're worth the risk.

Egg collectors go about their risky job in groups. One extremely brave man (generally speaking, women don't do this job) volunteers to do the collecting. He ties a rope around his middle while a small group of his friends hold the other end. He abseils down a 100-metre-high

cliff to collect the eggs, and then works his way back up again, collecting eggs as he goes.

Guillemots lay their eggs straight on to the tiny ledges in the cliff face. The egg collector puts the eggs into a bag tied around his waist, shooing away guillemots with his free hand. As well as the massive drop onto the rocks below, there are thousands of angry birds to deal with, but luckily the guillemots aren't too aggressive.

Viking Egg Collectors

The people of the Arctic are the only ones who still collect seabirds' eggs like this today. But in the past it was a lot more popular. The Vikings, for example, loved to eat seabirds' eggs (and seabirds too), and used to collect them in the same way as modern Arctic egg collectors. And in Great Britain, Guillemot eggs were collected from cliffs in Yorkshire until the beginning of the twentieth century.

Honey Hunters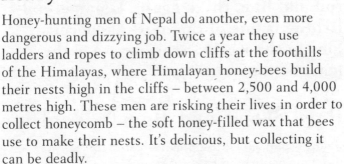

Honey-hunting men of Nepal do another, even more dangerous and dizzying job. Twice a year they use ladders and ropes to climb down cliffs at the foothills of the Himalayas, where Himalayan honey-bees build their nests high in the cliffs – between 2,500 and 4,000 metres high. These men are risking their lives in order to collect honeycomb – the soft honey-filled wax that bees use to make their nests. It's delicious, but collecting it can be deadly.

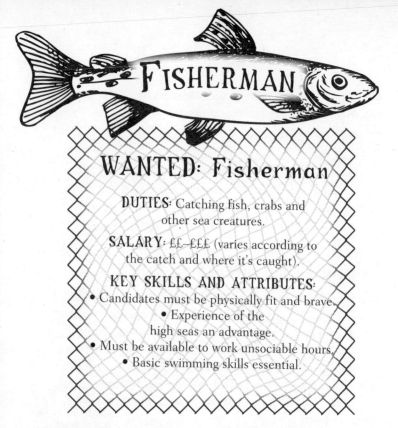

FISHERMAN

WANTED: Fisherman

DUTIES: Catching fish, crabs and other sea creatures.

SALARY: ££–£££ (varies according to the catch and where it's caught).

KEY SKILLS AND ATTRIBUTES:
- Candidates must be physically fit and brave.
- Experience of the high seas an advantage.
- Must be available to work unsociable hours.
- Basic swimming skills essential.

If you're thinking of sitting on a riverbank in the sunshine with a rod and line, think again. Commercial fishing is one of the most dangerous jobs in the world. Seasickness is the least of your worries . . .

Hard Work and Harsh Weather

Being a commercial fisherman is hard physical work, involving hauling up heavy nets and cages, sorting catches of slippery, smelly fish, and often having to work in the dead of night. In colder parts of the world, the weather can be a fisherman's worst enemy. Imagine struggling to keep your balance on an icy deck as the ship pitches and rolls in enormous waves. The danger of fishing boats being overturned and fishermen being crushed or washed overboard is always present.

Hazardous Crabs

Alaskan king crab fishing may be the most dangerous fishing job of all. Winter in the Bering Sea (which is when and where the Alaskan king crabs are caught) is freezing cold and very stormy. Because the crab-fishing season is so short (usually around four weeks), sometimes crab fishermen work for 20 hours non-stop to make the most of it.

Crab fishermen also run the risk of becoming tangled up in the lines attached to the crab pots or crushed by heavy machinery used for lifting the pots out of the water. Unlike many other fishermen, Alaskan crab fishermen can make a lot of money in a short period of time. But they face deadly peril in the process, and reports suggest that at least one crab fisherman dies every week during the crab-fishing season, usually from drowning or hypothermia.

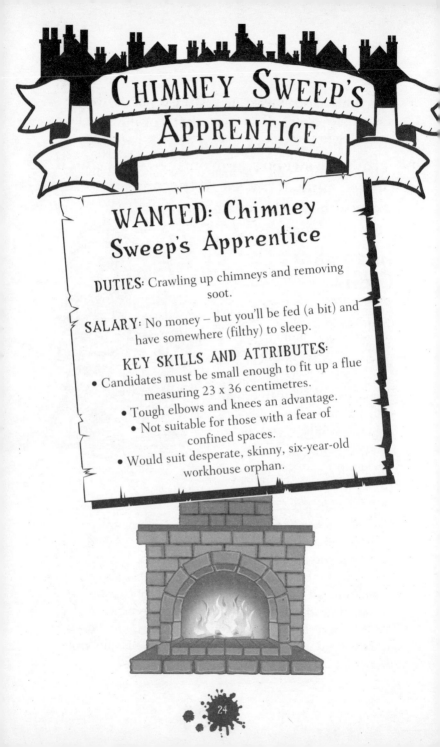

CHIMNEY SWEEP'S APPRENTICE

WANTED: Chimney Sweep's Apprentice

DUTIES: Crawling up chimneys and removing soot.

SALARY: No money – but you'll be fed (a bit) and have somewhere (filthy) to sleep.

KEY SKILLS AND ATTRIBUTES:

- Candidates must be small enough to fit up a flue measuring 23 x 36 centimetres.
- Tough elbows and knees an advantage.
- Not suitable for those with a fear of confined spaces.
- Would suit desperate, skinny, six-year-old workhouse orphan.

Chimney sweeps didn't used to have a great job – it wasn't very well paid, and it was extremely grimy. But a chimney sweep's apprentice had a much worse time. They were the ones who had to climb up the chimneys to do the actual sweeping.

Sooty Sweeps

From the 1600s onwards, houses were built with several fireplaces to keep them warm, each of which had a flue leading to a chimney pot. They had to be kept clean because chimneys that became full of soot could catch fire. Since the fireplaces were the main source of heat for most buildings, chimney sweeps were kept very busy.

Climbing Boys

Chimney sweeps employed apprentices, known as climbing boys. Because the job was hard, dirty and dangerous, climbing boys were usually so poor they had no other choice. Often climbing boys were recruited from workhouses – miserable places where the poorest people got food and lodging in return for horrible hard work like picking oakum (unpicking old bits of rope) or breaking stones.

Grim and Grimy

The climbing boys were forced to climb up even the narrowest of chimneys, armed with a brush to sweep down the soot as they went, and a scraper for tougher bits. Even though there were brushes available that could do the same job from 1803 onwards, chimney sweeps preferred to use boys – presumably they were cheaper and less trouble.

The boys had to be small and agile because the flues were very narrow, and they started young – at about the age of six. When they reached the top of the chimney, they had to climb back down, shovel the soot they'd removed into bags, and load it on to the sweep's cart. There was no pay, just somewhere to sleep with the other climbing boys, and some food (though the sweep would want to keep his boys nice and thin). As you can imagine, it was grim work. It was also very dangerous.

Horrible and Hazardous

Climbing boys suffered painfully scraped elbows and knees as they climbed the narrow chimneys, but that was the least of their worries. They had to put up with choking, poisonous soot and many suffered from asthma or other breathing difficulties as they grew up, as well as hunched backs from carrying bags of soot, inflamed eyes from the dirt and dust, and deformed joints from spending so much time in cramped spaces.

They also ran the risk of becoming trapped in a chimney and suffocating to death, or being burned if the chimney caught fire. As they grew up, many young sweeps suffered from a type of cancer caused by soot known as Chimney Sweeps' Cancer, which eventually killed them.

Sweeping Changes

In 1840 a law was passed making it illegal for anyone under 21 to climb a chimney, but most people ignored it. Children continued to be sent up chimneys, where many of them died, until 1875 in the UK. Today's chimney sweeps still use brushes, but now they use vacuum chimney cleaners as well, instead of young children.

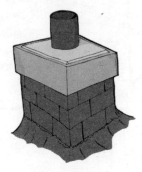

SOLDIER

WANTED: Soldier

DUTIES: Depend heavily on the circumstances, but will involve fighting (obviously). You could be shot at (with arrows, guns and other weapons), blown up, and possibly killed.

SALARY: ££–££££

KEY SKILLS AND ATTRIBUTES:
• Must be fit, brave and loyal.
• Ability to fit into a rigid hierarchy is essential (i.e. you have to be prepared to do whatever you're told).
• Relevant weapons training will be given.
• Would suit patriotic young men and women who are prepared to die for their country.

Being a soldier is, of course, highly dangerous. After all, soldiers are expected to fight in wars, which can prove fatal. However some wars have been especially dreadful for soldiers...

Napoleonic Soldiers

At the end of the 1700s and beginning of the 1800s, France was at war with lots of countries that wanted to put a stop to the French Revolution. The French leader was called Napoleon, so the conflicts were known as the Napoleonic Wars. When Napoleon first took control of the French Army, the soldiers had terrible equipment, poor quality clothing and not enough to eat. Napoleon tried to improve things for his men, but also he led thousands of them to their deaths in his ill-advised Russian Campaign.

In 1812 he led an army of 650,000 soldiers into Russia. They marched almost without stopping, along dry, dusty roads in the Russian summer. The Russian Army retreated, burning everything behind them. As a result, the exhausted French Army couldn't find any food or shelter. When the severe Russian winter began, the French troops froze. The Russians attacked when the French were at their weakest. Only 40,000 French soldiers managed to return to France.

The First World War

The First World War was fought from 1914–1918
between the Allies (Britain, France and Russia) and the
Central Powers (Germany, Austria-Hungary and Italy
– though things were complicated and Italy ended up
fighting for the Allies). In northern France and Belgium,
soldiers on each side of the war dug deep trenches in the
mud, facing one another, with a strip of desolate land
between the trenches to fight in, known as No Man's
Land. The line of trenches, known as the Western Front,
didn't move much throughout the entire war, despite
often fatal efforts on both sides. Conditions in the
trenches, where soldiers ate and slept, were appalling:
often cold and damp, and always filthy and rat-infested.
Sickness and disease were common. Both sides used

poison gas, which crept into the trenches and caused a painful, slow death for any soldiers who breathed it. Every so often, the order would come to go over the top of the trench to face the enemy – and probably be gunned down within seconds. Tens of thousands of young men could die in a single battle, and more than 10 million soldiers died in total during the war.

Troops Today

Modern soldiers don't dig trenches or march for thousands of miles in the freezing cold. Technology has changed the way wars are fought, but soldiers all over the world still have to face enemy soldiers, and the threat of ambushes, gunfire, landmines and bombs.

MINER

WANTED: Miner

DUTIES: Extracting coal, metal or precious stones from under the Earth's surface, often under extremely unpleasant and treacherous conditions.

SALARY: ££–££££

KEY SKILLS AND ATTRIBUTES:
- Must be strong, brave, and not afraid of the dark.
- Experience of using digging tools and/or heavy machinery an advantage.
- Not suitable for candidates who are afraid of confined spaces.
- Must be available for shift work (so that the mines can operate day and night).

Not many people would choose to spend their working day underground, especially not hundreds of metres underground, in dark, cramped conditions, where there's a high risk of exploding gas...

Prehistoric Pits

People have been mining since the Stone Age. In fact the oldest mine we know about is 43 thousand years old: at Lion Cave in Swaziland, people dug a tunnel into the rock to mine hematite, a red pigment used for decoration.

There are deeper ancient mines too – Grimes Graves at Brandon in eastern England is 14 metres deep, and it was dug to mine flint around 5,000 years ago. We don't know about the mining accidents that happened in those days, but there must have been some. We do know that mining became one of the world's most dangerous jobs as time went on.

Perilous Coal Pits

Mines have been dug all over the world since then, to bring up all sorts of things, including coal for fuel. Coal mining really got going in the industrial revolution in the nineteenth century, when new inventions meant that goods were produced in factories, and steam power, fuelled by coal, was used for machines and trains. In Britain, where the industrial revolution began, new coal mines were dug and communities sprang up around them. The work was hard, conditions were hot, damp, dark and filthy, and there was a risk of lung disease: coal miners (of the past and present) can develop various lung diseases as a result of breathing in coal dust. And in the nineteenth century there were plenty of jobs for children down the mines, pushing coal carts or opening traps (underground doorways) to let them through. Children as young as six would sit alone in the dark for hours, waiting to open a trap for a coal cart.

Fatal Firedamp

As if the awful conditions and diseases weren't enough, an even bigger danger in coal mines was firedamp, a flammable gas that lurks in underground pockets and can be difficult to detect. Explosions in underground mineshafts killed thousands of miners during the nineteenth century. In 1866, in one of the worst mining disasters in Britain, there was a gas explosion at the Oaks coal mine in South Yorkshire that killed 361 miners and 27 rescuers.

Twentieth Century Disasters

Although safety improved in mines, accidents still happened. The two worst mining disasters ever happened in the twentieth century. At the Courrières coal mine in northern France, 1,099 miners were killed in 1906 in a huge explosion, many of them children. At the Benixihu mine in China, which mined iron and coal, 1,549 miners died after a gas and coal dust explosion in 1942 – about a third of all the workers in the mine at the time.

Miners had other things to worry about too. At the Benixihu mine, which was controlled by Japan from the 1930s, Chinese labourers were forced to work underground in appalling conditions: they worked shifts of 12 hours and longer, they weren't given proper clothing to wear for the job, and deadly diseases such as typhoid and cholera were commonplace.

Modern Mining

Today, mining is still a job for only the bravest men and women. Every year hundreds of miners die around the world in mines. In 2010 there was a cave-in at a copper and gold mine in Chile, and 33 miners became trapped 700 metres underground, and five kilometres from the entrance to the mine. It took more than two months for rescuers to reach them, but eventually all 33 got out alive.

Mining Catastrophes from Around the World

Belgium: In the Bois-du Crazier mine in 1956, a fire caused when a mining cart hit an oil pipe and electricity lines trapped 262 miners underground. Only 12 survived.

Canada: In the Hillcrest mine disaster of 1914, an explosion caused by coal dust and methane killed 189 men and boys.

Chile: In 1945, 355 workers were killed after breathing in carbon monoxide at the El Teniente mine. It became known as 'The Smoke Tragedy'.

United States: In West Virginia in 1907 at the Monongah mine, a methane explosion killed 362 workers, including several men who suffocated during the rescue attempt.

Wales: Between 1850 and 1934, the South Wales Coalfield had the worst disaster record in the world. Multiple disasters at many different mines resulted in a total death toll of 3,119 people, either from explosions or suffocation.

Zimbabwe: In 1972 at the Wankie coal mine, 426 miners died after a series of explosions which released poisonous gas into the tunnels. Only three bodies were recovered.

36

COTTON MILL WORKER

WANTED: Cotton Mill Worker

DUTIES: Operating enormous, dangerous and noisy spinning machines.

SALARY: £–£££ (skilled workers are quite well paid, but many earn just about enough to keep them alive – until the machines or the poor working conditions kill them).

KEY SKILLS AND ATTRIBUTES:
- Experience not essential, though the more experience and skills you have, the higher your pay – *even* for women.
- Would suit ordinary working class men, women and children who live locally and don't have many other job options.

The industrial revolution completely changed the way people lived and worked. And it was responsible for the creation of a lot of new and very dangerous jobs.

City Living

In the eighteenth century, newly invented machines could do jobs like spinning and weaving much more efficiently than ever before. So instead of spinning or weaving in their own homes in the countryside, people went to live in towns and cities to operate machines in factories.

Housing for workers in the cities was very cramped: often a whole family had to live in just one room, and conditions were made even worse by poor sanitation, which led to disease. In the factories, where people spent most of their time (normal working hours were from six o'clock in the morning to eight o'clock in the evening), things didn't get any better...

Murderous Mills

Huge machines clattered constantly in the cotton mills. The machines were so noisy that workers became skilled lip-readers in order to communicate with one another, and many of them became deaf as a result of the loud noise. The machines were also dangerous (there weren't many safety regulations in the eighteenth and nineteenth centuries) and people regularly lost fingers, limbs or even their lives because of them.

The mills were kept hot (around 27°C) and damp to keep the cotton from breaking as it was spun – which might have been good for the cotton, but was very bad for the factory workers who had to work hard in the humidity and heat. Cotton dust led to eye infections, potentially fatal lung diseases, and particular types of cancer.

Mill Money

Pay wasn't too bad for the more highly skilled workers, but it was not nearly good enough to make up for the appalling working conditions. Many mill workers were paid partly in food and fuel for the fire instead of money; the goods came from the mill owner's warehouse, and the prices were fixed in favour of the owner (if the workers had been paid with money, they'd have been able to find their groceries cheaper elsewhere). The mills made a fortune for their owners, but the workers were generally badly paid, overworked and in constant danger of having serious accidents.

Jobs for Kids

The terrible conditions weren't just for grown-ups – there were plenty of jobs for children in the mills too, and they were paid far less than the adults. The smallest children, from the age of four, worked as 'scavengers'.

They had to crawl under the machinery to sweep away pieces of cotton fluff while the machines were still moving, risking being crushed or mangled. Often, if they didn't lie down flat enough as the machine moved over them, their hair would get caught and pulled out.

'Piecers' mended broken cotton threads by tying the broken strands together while the mechanical loom was still working. They had to be very quick to avoid getting hurt.

Modern Mills

Over time, better safety measures were brought in, and laws were passed to limit and eventually, stop children from working in factories. Trade unions were also formed to protect workers. New inventions and technology have made cotton mills a far less perilous place to work.

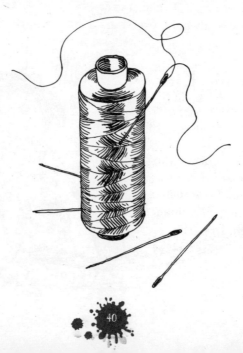

POWDER MONKEY

WANTED: Powder Monkey

DUTIES: Distributing gunpowder for the ship's cannons.

SALARY: £ (though there will be a share of the prize money if an enemy ship is captured).

KEY SKILLS AND ATTRIBUTES:
- Must be fast, agile, small, and brave.
- Not suitable for those with a fear of conflict or loud noises.
- Those who suffer from seasickness need not apply.
- Would suit young child with a taste for adventure, or small, fast adult.

In the eighteenth century, children who'd be at infant school today worked long and hard in all kinds of challenging and often perilous jobs. Powder monkeys, who worked on battleships, had one of the most dangerous jobs of all.

All Aboard

A navy ship in the eighteenth century wasn't a safe place to be. There were lots of diseases that could kill sailors; scurvy (caused by lack of vitamin C because there wasn't much fresh veg aboard ship), typhoid, malaria, yellow fever and cholera are just a small but horrifying selection.

In fact, disease accounted for more deaths among sailors than battles at sea. Accidents were common too; sailors might fall from the rigging, slip over on the deck or be washed overboard by a wave. The food was generally rock-hard and crawling with weevils and maggots.

Punishments were severe: minor crimes meant a good flogging with a nine-stranded whip called a cat o' nine tails, and serious crimes were punished with death. And when the ship went into battle, things got really bad...

Deadly Weapons

Navy ships' gundecks were armed with cannons, which used gunpowder to fire heavy iron cannonballs. The cannons were very dangerous – and not just to enemy ships. When they were fired, cannons would shoot backwards on their wheels with the force of the blast, so they were restrained with ropes, which sometimes broke. The cannonballs had to be secured so that they didn't roll around on the gundeck, causing a lethal hazard. And the gunpowder used to fire the cannons had a habit of exploding.

Cannon Crew

Each cannon needed a team of six sailors to fire it, including the powder monkey, each with particular responsibilities. The powder monkey's job was to run from the mayhem of the gundeck – negotiating the firing cannons, enemy fire, splintering wood and severely injured sailors – as fast as he (or, in some cases, she) could down long, narrow gangways to the magazine, where the gunpowder was stored.

Gunpowder couldn't be left anywhere near the cannons because a stray spark could easily make the whole lot blow up. The gunner (the sailor in charge of ammunition in the magazine) would pass the powder monkey a cartridge of gunpowder through a wet curtain, which was there to keep out heat and sparks.

Once the powder monkey had the gunpowder in his hands, he had to run as fast as he could back to the gundeck in order to supply his cannon team with more firepower, desperately hoping that the gunpowder didn't ignite on the way. If it did, chances of survival were next to none.

Disgusting Jobs

Have you ever considered a career
sniffing armpits or shovelling poo?
There are plenty of disgusting
occupations to choose from...

GONG FARMER

WANTED: Gong Farmer

DUTIES: Cleaning out cess pits and toilet chutes.

SALARY: £ (Not nearly enough!)

KEY SKILLS AND ATTRIBUTES:

- Candidates must be strong and handy with a shovel.
- Total lack of **a)** squeamishness and **b)** sense of smell both definite advantages.
- Must relish a hands-on approach.
- Must be available to work nights.

It's hard to think of a more revolting job than being a gong farmer! Before sewers became commonplace, there was only one way to get rid of poo, and that was to shovel it up and carry it away.

Early Toilets

In the days before toilets, people would use a pot or a bucket. The contents would then be thrown out of the window, or collected in a pit. Early toilets were wooden seats over pits of waste (cess pits), usually outside the house. The contents of the pit could then be spread on the fields as a smelly but useful fertiliser for crops, or it could just stay there, and wait for someone to take it away when the pit became full.

Buckets and Shovels

That's where the gong farmer came in, because his job was to empty the pit when it was full (usually to the point of overflowing). The beginning of the job was absolutely disgusting, and it got steadily worse from there. The liquid would collect on the top of the pile, so the first step was to remove all the wet waste using a bucket.

Then the gong farmer would start shovelling out the solid stuff, which got more and more compact the lower down he dug. Once he'd finished, he'd take his stinking vat of human waste off by horse and cart and dump it in the nearest river. And, by the way, the gong farmer would have to do his dirty job under cover of darkness – no one wanted to see, or smell the inside of a cess pit, so he had to do it when everyone else was asleep.

Castle Gong Farmers

Castle toilets were little rooms that jutted out over the side of the castle, called garderobes, which is where we get the word 'wardrobe' from today, as people used to hang their good set of clothes in there in the hope that the bad smells would keep the moths away. They didn't seem to mind about wearing clothes that smelled bad.

The waste went straight down the side of the castle and landed in the moat. Or, if there wasn't a moat, it collected in a large, steaming pile. It was the gong farmer's job to clean the garderobe chutes, and get rid of the big pile of poo at the bottom of the castle walls (once it had mounted up nicely).

Disgusting *and* Dangerous

A gong farmer's job was incredibly smelly, totally disgusting and could also be fatal. Rotting poo gives off hydrogen sulphide, a highly flammable gas that smells like rotten eggs. Breathing in hydrogen sulphide in a confined space (such as a cess pit, for example), can kill.

Modern Gong Farmers

No one farms gongs any more, but plenty of people clean toilets. Modern sewers make it a much less disgusting job than a gong farmer's, though. The closest modern equivalent of a gong farmer today is a sewer cleaner. In India, for example, sewer cleaners often have to climb down narrow manholes into the sewer system to unblock pipes manually, and sometimes they end up covered in human waste!

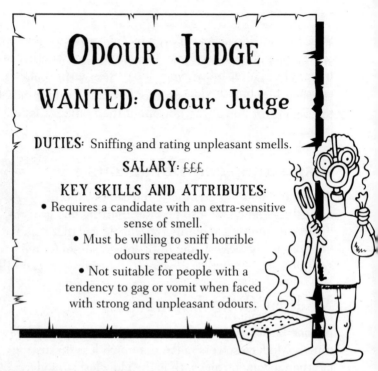

Odour Judge

WANTED: Odour Judge

DUTIES: Sniffing and rating unpleasant smells.

SALARY: £££

KEY SKILLS AND ATTRIBUTES:
- Requires a candidate with an extra-sensitive sense of smell.
- Must be willing to sniff horrible odours repeatedly.
- Not suitable for people with a tendency to gag or vomit when faced with strong and unpleasant odours.

You've probably never considered smelling things as a career, but just as with food tasting, it turns out there are all sorts of unpleasant smells that need judging.

Whiffy Work

Which would you rather sniff: a sweaty armpit, bad breath, cat litter, smelly socks, bad eggs, or farts? Your answer is probably, 'none of them!', but some people with especially sensitive noses make a living from sniffing bad smells like these.

Sensitive sniffers are employed by companies to find out, for example, how effective a deodorant is, or whether one brand of cat litter hides the smell of cat poo better than another. Bad breath sniffers are employed by mouthwash companies.

Fart Judge

A US scientist who studies stomach problems, with a specialism in farting, conducted an experiment involving two odour judges: 16 adults farted down a tube into a container, providing more than a hundred samples.

The two odour judges then had to sniff each container, rating how bad the smell was. The scientist was then able to work out which gas is the smelliest part of a human fart (if you're interested, it's hydrogen sulphide – yes, the same flammable gas that could kill gong farmers!) It might well have been the worst odour-judging job of all time.

TOSHER

WANTED: Tosher

DUTIES: Searching the sewers for valuables.

SALARY: £££

KEY SKILLS AND ATTRIBUTES:
- Candidates must be willing to get their hands (and everything else) dirty.
- Own lamp and pole essential.
- Knowledge of the tides in the River Thames, London a definite advantage.
- Would suit strong, able-bodied man (no women need apply).

The toshers of Victorian London could make a decent living out of sifting through raw sewage. But would you do it, even if it made you a millionaire?

Smelly London

After the Great Stink of London in 1858, when the River Thames stank so badly that the politicians could no longer bear the smell, the government decided that something had to be done with the sewage of London that didn't involve chucking it straight into the River Thames.

So a huge and complicated network of sewers was built to take it away . . . and chuck it into the River Thames, but closer to the sea where the politicians didn't have to smell it. As well as making the Thames less smelly, the new sewers provided a new job opportunity.

Toshing

It wasn't only poo and wee that ended up in the sewers: there might be pieces of metal that could be gathered together and sold, and the odd coin, or even jewellery, dropped down a drain by mistake. Obviously, what ended up in the sewers was *mostly* poo and wee, and you'd have to wade through an enormous amount of it before you found anything valuable. But, if you were prepared to do an incredibly disgusting job, you could usually find enough of value to earn a living.

Toshers *were* prepared to do the job. They spent their days poking about in the stench and the dark, using a two-metre-long pole with a hoe on the end to poke through the sewage and a lamp strapped to their backs to help them see in the gloom. A tosher might smell dreadful, but he could earn quite a good living out of his disgusting job.

Deadly Drains

As well as the overwhelming stench and filth, there were other downsides to the job. Sewer rats could be dangerous, and so could the fumes from the sewage, especially in hot weather. The tides and wet weather meant that toshers sometimes drowned in the sewers. And, of course, there were about a gazillion germs all over the place, so toshers were lucky if they didn't catch a deadly disease.

Mudlarks

Mudlarks did a similar job to the toshers, but their job was possibly even worse. They searched the banks of the Thames at low tide for anything of value, and were usually children, both boys and girls, who had no other way of getting money to pay for food.

They weren't just searching through mud, but human sewage too. Barefoot, they ran the risk of being cut by broken glass and nails. Unlike most toshers, they barely managed to scavenge enough to feed themselves.

Find out about other horrible Victorian jobs, such as being a chimney sweep's apprentice, on page 24.

GROOM OF THE STOOL

WANTED: Groom of the Stool

DUTIES: Attending His Majesty the King in his 'most personal' acts.

SALARY: £££££

KEY SKILLS AND ATTRIBUTES:
- Candidates must be of noble birth.
- They must also be absolutely trustworthy, and not afraid to get their hands dirty.
- Would suit ambitious fawning male aristocrat.
- Poor sense of smell an advantage.

If you were a Tudor King of England, you weren't expected to just go to the toilet like everyone else. Instead, a huge fuss was made of the whole process, and it required a special servant: the Groom of the Stool.

The Royal Toilet

The Groom of the Stool's job title came from the 'close stool', which was a sort of portable toilet, padded like a comfy chair, with a bucket underneath. This was where the royal poo would be produced. Today, 'stool' is another word for a poo.

Royal Behinds

The Groom of the Stool would help the king get dressed and undressed, and wait while the king sat his enormous (at least in Henry VIII's case) bottom on the close stool and went about his business, perhaps making polite conversation while he did so. Then – the most important part of the job – the Groom of the Stool would wipe the king's behind, using only the finest cotton and a bowl of water, and dry it with a towel. The poo itself was then shown to a team of doctors, who inspected it for signs of the king's health.

Posh Grooms

Whoever had the task of assisting the king on the toilet, it had to be someone the king trusted and felt comfortable with, so the job was seen as an important privilege. The Groom of the Stool would have been a very posh man, who was extremely well paid for his services, and would probably go on to have an even more important job in the royal court. The job was abolished by Queen Elizabeth I – she had a First Lady of the Bedchamber instead.

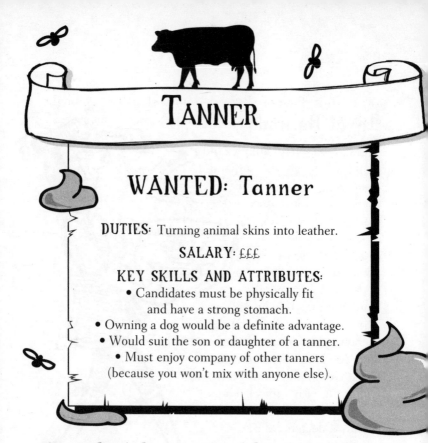

TANNER

WANTED: Tanner

DUTIES: Turning animal skins into leather.

SALARY: £££

KEY SKILLS AND ATTRIBUTES:
- Candidates must be physically fit and have a strong stomach.
- Owning a dog would be a definite advantage.
- Would suit the son or daughter of a tanner.
- Must enjoy company of other tanners (because you won't mix with anyone else).

Leather's been around for thousands of years and we still use it for lots of things today. The process of making it used to be hard work, messy, and very, very smelly (and it still is in some places).

Soaking Skins

The process of tanning smelled so bad that tanneries were always on the outskirts of towns, so that people who didn't work there didn't have to put up with the awful whiff. First of all, fresh animal skins were brought to the tannery from abattoirs and butchers. They were washed and trimmed, then they were put in a pit containing lime and (often) urine.

In Roman times, the wee was sometimes collected in pots on street corners (so passing wee-ers could use it and give the tanners free supplies at the same time). This smelly soak removed most of the flesh, fat and fur from the skins.

Pits of Poo

The tanners then had to scrape off the fur, rotting flesh and fat using a big knife. It was hard physical labour, and a horrible, sticky, smelly process. But worse was to come. The de-furred skins were put into another pit to get rid of the lime and make the skins softer. This pit contained . . . poo. Preferably dog poo, which apparently works best, but also pigeon poo, and perhaps a few animal brains. (In fact, collecting dog poo was a whole job in itself – dog poo gatherers were called Pure Collectors, and they supplied the tanneries with their horrible hoard.)

Once they'd stewed nicely for a while in the poo mixture, the skins were soaked in tanning fluid for several months. You'll be pleased to know that the tanning fluid didn't contain brains, poo or wee, but bark chippings, which contain chemicals called tannins.

What a Whiff

No wonder the tanneries smelled so bad: the unholy stench was a combination of animal blood, rotting flesh and fat, urine and dog poo. Leather can be made by less smelly methods nowadays, using machines and man-made chemicals rather than dog poo.

But there are places around the world where the old-fashioned tanning methods are still used. These tanneries are still on the outskirts of town, and they're still some of the stinkiest places in the world.

For more about people who collected poo for a living, go to page 46.

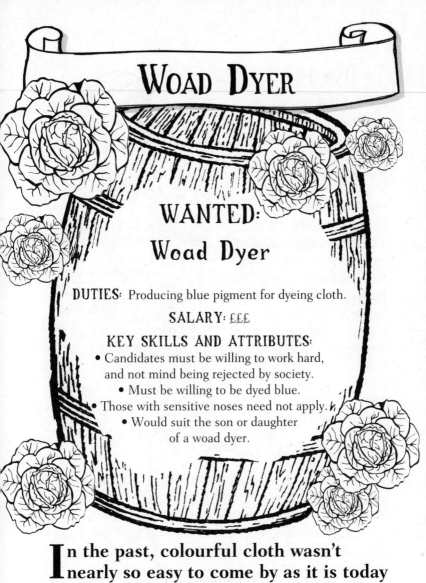

WOAD DYER

WANTED:
Woad Dyer

DUTIES: Producing blue pigment for dyeing cloth.

SALARY: £££

KEY SKILLS AND ATTRIBUTES:
- Candidates must be willing to work hard,
  and not mind being rejected by society.
- Must be willing to be dyed blue.
- Those with sensitive noses need not apply.
- Would suit the son or daughter
  of a woad dyer.

In the past, colourful cloth wasn't
nearly so easy to come by as it is today
– it was a long and difficult process and,
in the case of blue dye, an extremely
smelly one.

To Dye For

Until the 1600s, woad was the only source of blue dye in Europe. Woad is a plant from the cabbage family, and its leaves produce the dye, which has been used since the Stone Age. There were woad-growing areas in France, Germany, Italy and England and, because blue dye was in high demand, it was an expensive crop that made some Medieval woad growers very rich. But growing it was a lot easier than turning it into dye.

Woad Whiff

The woad was chopped up into bits and made into a paste (sometimes using a horse-driven mill), then shaped into balls by hand and left to dry for a few weeks. Then the hard balls were broken up, sprinkled with water and left to ferment. None of this sounds too bad, until you consider that the woad gave off a really terrible smell while it was fermenting (like boiled cabbage, only a lot worse). And the next part of the process was even stinkier...

A Royal Stink

The woad was put into barrels, which were then filled with hot water. Wood ash or urine was also added, and after a few days of soaking the woad was ready to be used to dye cloth. Even if wood ash was used instead of urine, the smell was absolutely foul – like a cess pit with rotten Brussels sprouts thrown in.

Queen Elizabeth I must have caught a whiff of it at some point, because she made it a rule that there was to be no woad dyeing within five miles (eight kilometers) of her royal person.

Lonely Dyers

Woad dyers made a fairly decent living from their work, but they paid for it in more ways than just hard work and getting used to the pong. Because of the terrible smell, woad dyers ended up isolated from other people, in small communities on the outskirts of town where not many people could smell them and their whiffy trade – just like tanners. Even after a good hot bath it was possible to tell a woad dyer, because the dye would turn the dyers' hands blue.

End of the Woad

Eventually, as trade routes opened to the East, woad was gradually replaced by indigo, which is also a plant dye but isn't nearly so smelly. Today synthetic dyes mean that no one has to suffer for blue dye as they did in the past.

FARTING ENTERTAINER

WANTED: Farting Entertainer

DUTIES: Farting in an entertaining manner.

SALARY: £££–£££££

KEY SKILLS AND ATTRIBUTES:
- Candidates must be hilariously funny and totally uninhibited.
- The ability to produce loud and/or musical farts at will is essential.
- The ability to fart out candles is a strong advantage.
- Fondness for toilet humour preferable.

You either think farting is funny or you don't. Apparently there have always been enough people around who find it absolutely hilarious for professional farting entertainers – or 'flatulists' – to make a living.

Roland the Farter

Farting jesters go back to the fifth century, and probably earlier than that. In the Middle Ages, King Henry II of England employed a jester known as Roland the Farter. When Roland retired, he was given a manor house with 30 acres of land in Suffolk as a retirement present from the King – but he was still required to turn up and amuse the King with his special brand of humour every Christmas Day. King John of England also employed a farting entertainer, a Frenchman known as Peter the Farter.

Le Petomane

Joseph Pujol, known as Le Petomane (meaning 'fart maniac') was another French farter. At the end of the nineteenth century he was the world's most highly paid entertainer – the equivalent of Jay-Z, except with wind. He entertained audiences by farting tunes and blowing candles out with his bottom.

Mr Methane

Farting entertainers are still around today. Paul Oldfield from the United Kingdom is better known as Mr Methane. He entertains audiences in a similar way to Le Petomane, more than 100 years before – but, unlike him, Mr Methane has produced CDs and DVDs. He appeared on Britain's got Talent, where judge Simon Cowell called him a 'disgusting creature', but the judges liked him better in Germany: he made it to the semi-finals on the German version of the TV show.

POISONOUS JOBS

Some of the world's worst jobs
resulted in a slow, painful death by
poisoning – though the people
doing the jobs didn't realise
that at the time…

Hat Maker

These days, hats are made without poisoning anybody, but in the past the job was highly toxic, causing horrible side effects and sometimes even death.

WANTED: HAT MAKER

DUTIES: Making felt hats.

SALARY: ££–£££

KEY SKILLS AND ATTRIBUTES:
- Skilled craftspeople will have a strong advantage, though training will be given.
- Preference will be given to candidates who don't make a fuss about strange and unpleasant physical symptoms.
- Willingness to work in stuffy, smelly environment essential.

Carroting Hats

From the 1600s to the 1900s, most men's hats were made from felt. The felt was made by soaking animal fur in mercury nitrate, a chemical that made the fur softer and easier to work with. The process, called 'carroting'

because the liquid was orange-coloured, began in France in the 1600s, and made its way to other parts of the world, including Britain and the United States.

During carroting, workers would breathe in the fumes from the liquid, especially in factories that weren't well ventilated. Before mercury nitrate was used, the fur was soaked in urine – which sounds pretty awful, but actually was an awful lot better for the hat makers. Hats were much more popular in the past than they are today, so felt hat makers were kept very busy indeed.

Hazardous Hats

Unfortunately for the hat makers, mercury is extremely poisonous. The hatters breathed in the toxic fumes from carroting and ended up with some or all of the horrible symptoms of mercury poisoning: headaches, trembling hands, facial ticks, blackened teeth, slurred speech and memory loss.

Eventually the mercury could damage hat makers' brains so badly that they would see things that weren't there, and behave in very odd ways. Mercury can also damage the kidneys and muscles, and in the worse cases, can kill.

The Shakes

Hat makers used mercury for carroting for around 300 years, despite the dreadful risks. In Danbury, Connecticut in the US, the hatting industry began at the end of the 1700s and continued into the twentieth century, when there were 56 hat-making factories supplying millions of hats every year.

Nearly half of the workers had signs of mercury poisoning, known as the Danbury Shakes. The first laws protecting hatters from mercury nitrate poisoning were passed in France at the end of the 1800s. In the United States, the use of mercury in the hatting industry wasn't banned until 1941.

HAZMAT DIVER

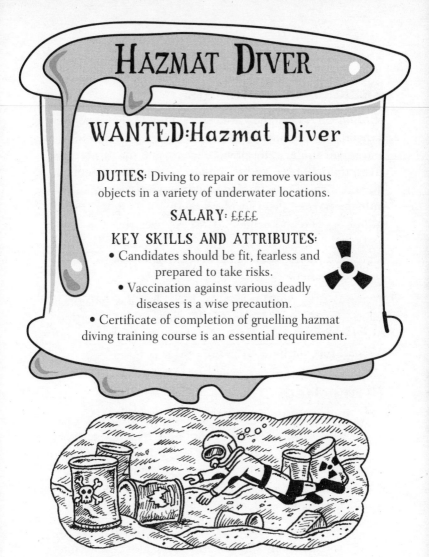

WANTED: Hazmat Diver

DUTIES: Diving to repair or remove various objects in a variety of underwater locations.

SALARY: ££££

KEY SKILLS AND ATTRIBUTES:
- Candidates should be fit, fearless and prepared to take risks.
- Vaccination against various deadly diseases is a wise precaution.
- Certificate of completion of gruelling hazmat diving training course is an essential requirement.

If you're imagining diving in clear water with loads of tropical fish darting about, you're on the wrong track. Hazmat is short for hazardous material...

Hazardous Materials

Hazmat divers find themselves in some of the most dangerous situations possible. It's their job to maintain and repair underwater pipes, sewers, and machinery, to clean up pollution, and to recover underwater objects including dead bodies. For example, a job for one unlucky hazmat diver involved diving in a pig farm lake full of pig poo and urine and old syringes that the farmer had used to give the pigs injections, in order to fix tow ropes to a tractor that had fallen into the lake so that it could be pulled out.

The next time you think you've had a bad day, imagine swimming through pig poo while dodging syringes that could pierce your wetsuit and put you in direct contact with all sorts of hideous germs.

Diving Gear

As well as sharp objects and animal waste, hazmat divers might have to dive in water containing toxic chemicals, or in water where there are nets and other hazards that could trap them. As the pig farm lake example shows, hazmat divers sometimes find it very difficult to see when they're diving, adding to the danger.

To protect them, divers wear strong drysuits (which means the diver remains dry inside the suit), sometimes with extra protection over the top of the drysuit to protect it from punctures. Divers also wear helmets, through which they can communicate with people on the surface, and thick gloves and boots.

Sewer Diving

The sewers of Mexico City have a tough job to do, because the city they're supposed to drain is sitting on top of a natural underground well. To make sure the city doesn't flood, two divers have the even tougher job of maintaining and unblocking the city's sewers.

They regularly dive through a mixture of human waste and toxic gases given off by rubbish to make repairs, remove debris, and retrieve the bodies of rotting dead animals and even murder victims. Swimming through the horrible, poisonous sludge, the sewer divers can't see anything and have to feel their way along.

MATCH MAKER

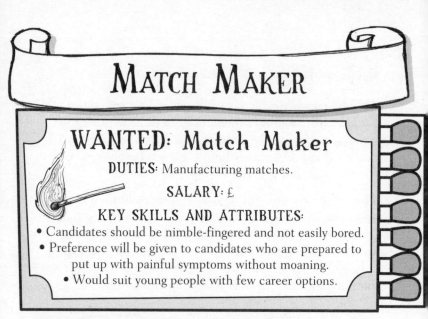

WANTED: Match Maker

DUTIES: Manufacturing matches.

SALARY: £

KEY SKILLS AND ATTRIBUTES:
- Candidates should be nimble-fingered and not easily bored.
- Preference will be given to candidates who are prepared to put up with painful symptoms without moaning.
- Would suit young people with few career options.

Today matches are made by machines in factories, but they used to be made by hand. And it was an extremely toxic process...

Bright Sparks

Before matches the business of lighting a fire could be time-consuming and complicated, so once matches were invented in the nineteenth century they were very, very popular. Unfortunately for the people who made matches, the chemical that made matches work – white phosphorus – was very poisonous.

Phossy Jaw

In the nineteenth and early twentieth centuries, matches were made by dipping wooden sticks into white phosphorous, often in cramped, airless rooms. The men, women and children who made the matches often developed a horrible disease called phosphorous necrosis, or 'phossy jaw', from breathing in vapours from the white phosphorus, which made people's jawbones crumble.

First the workers got a toothache, followed by swollen gums, abscesses and an awful-smelling discharge. The rotting jaw would actually glow in the dark! Eventually the victims died. If it was caught early enough, removing a few teeth might save the patient, but if it was left, the whole jawbone would have to be removed – and even then the patient might still die.

It was horrible, painful and disfiguring. Since people had to pay to be treated by a doctor in those days, and since match makers weren't paid very much, there was a strong possibility of the disease becoming life-threatening.

Safety Matches

A safer type of phosphorous was found and used by some manufacturers, but not all of them. Amazingly, some companies continued to use the deadly white phosphorous, even though it was known to kill and disfigure workers, because the alternative was more expensive.

Modern Matches

White phosphorous hasn't been used to make matches for nearly a hundred years. Today matches aren't made by hand, and the chemicals used aren't dangerous to the people who work in the factories or anyone lighting a match.

RADIUM DIAL PAINTER

WANTED:
Radium Dial Painter

DUTIES: Painting watch hands and other objects with radioactive paint to make them glow in the dark.

SALARY: ££

KEY SKILLS AND ATTRIBUTES:
- Candidates must have good eyesight.
- Patience, accuracy and attention to detail are essential skills.
- Would suit young women.
- Anyone likely to incite unrest among the workforce need not apply.

Painting the hands on watch faces for a living doesn't sound too bad. Unfortunately, the paint used in the past to make watch hands glow in the dark was deadly...

76

Radiant Radium

Radium is a radioactive chemical element discovered by Marie Curie in 1898. She also made the discovery that her new element glowed in the dark. Not long afterwards a radium-based luminous paint was invented, which could be used on watch dials, clocks and other instrument dials.

Not only did this mean that no one had to turn the light on at night in order to tell the time, but instrument dials on planes and other vehicles and machinery could be clearly seen in low light. The first big company to make dials painted with radium opened in New Jersey in the US, in 1914 – just in time for the First World War, which meant there was a big demand for the instrument dials.

Poisonous Paint

The radium dial painters, mostly young women, mixed glue, water and radium powder and applied it to dials with paint brushes. Because the work was very precise, they often licked the end of the brush to make a fine point. This meant that the workers were absorbing radium into their bodies at an extremely dangerous rate.

The painters soon became ill with 'radium jaw' – a disease similar to 'phossy jaw' (see page 75) – as well as bone cancer, and lots of other horrible symptoms associated with radiation poisoning. From the 1920s, radium dial painters began to die while they were still young. Hundreds of young women died as a result of this poisonous job.

Court Case

A group of female radium painters working in New Jersey took the company they worked for to court in the 1920s. During the trial evidence was shown that the owners of the company, Radium Corporation, and the scientists who worked there, took care to protect themselves from the effects of radium, but didn't bother protecting the workers, or even telling them that putting the paintbrushes in their mouths was harmful.

The company tried to cover up the harmful effects on the factory workers, and tried to pretend that any deaths were caused by other diseases, not by exposure to radium.

Despite the court case, none of the women or their families received much compensation. However, after the 1920s workers were protected by new health and safety laws and dial painting was made much safer. Today's luminous dial hands don't use paint that's harmfully radioactive.

MEDICAL EXPERIMENT TEST SUBJECT

WANTED: Medical Experiment Test Subject

DUTIES: To undergo a wide variety of unpleasant and possibly dangerous medical procedures.

SALARY: £–££ (or sometimes nothing at all).

KEY SKILLS AND ATTRIBUTES:
- Candidates must be human.
- Some interesting medical problems could be an advantage.
- Selfless commitment to the common good is a strong advantage.
- Would suit an unselfish risk-taker.

Medical experiments on human beings have been happening for a long, long time. Back in the Stone Age, someone had to be the first person to have their tooth drilled for a filling (the first one we know about was in the Indus Valley about 9,000 years ago). But they probably didn't get paid for it.

Smallpox Cure

One of the most famous medical experiments was carried out by the doctor Edward Jenner: he injected an eight-year-old boy called James Phipps with the not very dangerous disease cowpox in the hope that it would make the boy immune to the extremely deadly disease smallpox.

Luckily, after infecting the boy with smallpox about six weeks later, Jenner discovered he was right, and from then on people could be vaccinated against smallpox, bringing an end to the disease.

Guinea Pigs

Back then, other groups who would have found it difficult to say no to medical experiments were used too – prisoners, mentally ill hospital patients, soldiers (who had to obey their officers) and prisoners of war.

People have been injected with deadly diseases and toxic chemicals in medical experiments, and quite a few have died as a result, whether they volunteered and were paid, or not.

Nowadays medical testing isn't quite as dangerous as it was in the past, although sometimes people do still die. Without willing human test subjects however, new cures might not be found for diseases that kill millions of people every year.

GORY JOBS

Battlefield blood and guts,
amputated limbs, and disembodied
heads stuck on poles are all in a day's
work for some people. These jobs
are not for the squeamish!

BARBER-SURGEON

WANTED:
Barber-Surgeon

DUTIES: Cutting hair, shaving, pulling teeth, blood-letting, limb amputation and general surgery.

SALARY: ££££ (but varies according to experience and number of wealthy clients).

KEY SKILLS AND ATTRIBUTES:
- Knowledge of blood-letting essential.
- Other medical knowledge desirable but not necessary.
- Must be prepared to ignore blood-curdling screams.
- Own saw, scissors, knives and other surgical instruments an advantage.

Barber-surgeons were hairdressers, dentists and doctors all rolled into one. The hairdressing bit was the only aspect of the job that didn't involve lots of blood. At least, not often...

Beards and Teeth

The most common type of doctors in the Middle Ages (between the fifth and fifteenth centuries) were barber-surgeons. They had a varied job: they might give someone a short back and sides and a beard trim in the morning, then amputate someone's leg in the afternoon. They could also pull teeth out, which was the most successful cure for a toothache in those days.

A Sense of Humour

Medical knowledge at the time in Europe was a bit . . . primitive. It was based on the teachings of an ancient Greek doctor called Hippocrates, but sadly he'd got one or two things wrong. According to Hippocrates, human

health depended on a balance of four different 'humours' – if a patient was ill, it meant that he or she had too much or too little of one or more of the humours.

To make a diagnosis, the barber-surgeon would make a careful study of the patient's urine – by looking at it, sniffing it and even tasting it. The most common form of treatment, which seemed to be the cure for most things, was blood-letting. The barber-surgeon would either bleed the patient using a special tool to pierce the skin and let the blood out, or use his trusty jar of hungry leeches.

Chop Chop

Sometimes more drastic measures were needed. Barber-surgeons might be called on to deal with mangled limbs, and would be ready, with a nice sharp saw and a needle and thread, to chop them off. It was messy and very, very painful, and the closest thing to an anaesthetic was lots and lots of alcohol to numb the senses.

Barbers, Doctors and Dentists

As time went on, barber-surgeons weren't allowed to perform surgery such as amputating limbs, which was taken over by medical physicians, although a bit of teeth-pulling and blood-letting was all right. Eventually, hairdressing, dentistry and medical surgery became quite separate, which was probably just as well.

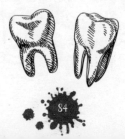

EXECUTIONER

WANTED:

Executioner

DUTIES: Hanging, beheading, burning, torturing and other assorted punishments.

SALARY: ££££

KEY SKILLS AND ATTRIBUTES:
- Candidates must be strong, grim-faced and utterly ruthless
- People with no friends, or those willing to become social outcasts preferred.
- Axe and/or sword skills an advantage.
- Must be willing to kill men, women and sometimes children on command.

The ultimate punishment for crime has always been death, and the death penalty can't be enforced without executioners. Throughout history there have always been people willing to do this gruesome job.

Modern Executions

Around 60 countries still sentence prisoners to the death penalty today, and people are still hanged, beheaded and even stoned to death, as well as more modern methods of execution, such as electrocution or injection with a lethal drug. In 2011 there were 676 documented executions in 20 countries around the world (though some countries keep details of their executions a secret, so the real number is probably much higher).

Especially Horrible Executions

In the past, methods of execution were sometimes even more horrible than they are today. As well as hanging and beheading, there was boiling, burning, sawing in half . . . the list goes on and on. Before being killed, a person might suffer all sorts of cruel tortures too.

In ancient Rome, someone who had killed his or her own father would be sentenced to die in an unusual way: they would be put into a sack with a cockerel, a snake, a monkey and a dog, then the sack was sealed up and thrown into the River Tiber.

Hanging, drawing and quartering was the punishment reserved for treason (plotting against a king or queen) – it meant dragging the prisoner to the gallows tied to a horse (drawing), hanging him until nearly dead, disembowelling him, then cutting his head off and dividing the body into quarters.

The four quarters would then be displayed – which was yet another unpleasant aspect of an executioner's job. He would prepare body parts for display – for example in

87

England, heads were often displayed on London Bridge, and it would be the executioner's job to boil the head, and perhaps pickle it to preserve it, before sticking it on a pike and displaying it.

Excluded Executioners

The job was extremely gruesome, and often very cruel, and it's difficult to imagine who would be willing to do it. It's not surprising that executioners were often shunned by the rest of society. For example, in the Ottoman Empire, executioners were kept separate from everyone else and were even buried in their own graveyards.

Revenge

As well as all the blood, guts and general horror, plus the possibility of becoming a social outcast, the executioner's job could be dangerous too – friends of an executed person might want to take their revenge on the executioner. When Charles I was executed in 1649 after the Second English Civil War, the executioner refused the job and an anonymous substitute was found instead.

CRIMEAN WAR NURSE

WANTED: Nurse

DUTIES: Caring for the sick in a filthy army hospital in the middle of a war zone.

SALARY: Trained nurses: £
Nuns: nothing at all.

KEY SKILLS AND ATTRIBUTES:

• Applicants must be either a trained hospital nurse or a nun (in which case no experience is necessary).
• Must be clean, methodical and up to Miss Nightingale's high standards.
• The squeamish need not apply.
• Must be willing to risk catching a wide variety of deadly diseases.

A nurse's job today might sometimes be bloody, but nurses do their jobs because they want to help sick and injured people. In the past, and during one war in particular, nurses worked hard in terrible conditions which unfortunately made their patients worse rather than better...

Death and Disease

Britain, France and their allies fought Russia in the Crimean War from 1853 to 1856. Disease raged through the troops, especially cholera and malaria, and if the soldiers needed hospital treatment they found themselves in a filthy army hospital, where soldiers were more likely to die of disease than war wounds (only one in six deaths in Crimean army hospitals were because of war injuries).

Florence Nightingale, who's become one of the most famous nurses in history, organised a team of 38 nurses and went to the Crimea (a peninsula to the south of Ukraine) to help.

Horrible Hospitals

The nurses found things were even worse than they'd imagined. There was hardly any medicine, the soldiers, their clothing and their beds were dirty and lice-infested, and infections and diseases such as typhus, typhoid and dysentery were killing the wounded.

Florence Nightingale pleaded with the British government to send help, and all the nurses worked as hard as they could to improve things, in the middle of the blood, gore and dirt, exposing themselves to the same diseases that were killing the soldiers. Some of them died.

Even More Death and Disease

Florence Nightingale didn't realise that the main cause of disease and infection were the sewers, which weren't working properly, the ventilation, which was poor and allowed diseases to spread quickly, and overcrowding. She thought the soldiers were dying in such numbers because of a lack of food and supplies, and because the nurses were overworked.

Despite the best efforts of Florence Nightingale and the other nurses, the death rate in the hospital began to rise, and became the highest of all the hospitals in the region. The British government sent a Sanitary Commission to the hospital, which improved the sewers and ventilation, and the death rate fell dramatically.

Because of her horrific experience in the Crimea, Florence Nightingale spent the rest of her life campaigning for better conditions in hospitals. She did end up improving things, and founded a nursing school in London.

Nursing on the Battlefield

Mary Seacole was another nurse who went to the Crimea to help the wounded. She came from Jamaica, where she'd had lots of experience of treating cholera, but even so her help was refused by the British government.

She made the journey to the Crimea at her own expense, and raised money by running a café so that she could buy supplies and nurse the wounded and sick. She nursed the soldiers on the battlefield, rather than inside a hospital – so as well as risking disease, Mary Seacole risked being blown to bits as well.

HORRIBLE JOBS

You definitely wouldn't want a job that's boring, badly paid, painful and repetitive, but millions of people have suffered these absolutely horrible jobs in the past, and some still do…

COTTON PICKER

Harvesting plants might sound like a fun job in the fresh air, but most picking jobs are very hard work and pay very little money. Picking cotton might just be the worst of the lot.

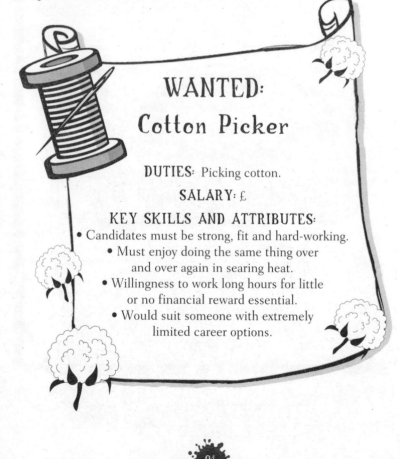

WANTED:

Cotton Picker

DUTIES: Picking cotton.

SALARY: £

KEY SKILLS AND ATTRIBUTES:
- Candidates must be strong, fit and hard-working.
- Must enjoy doing the same thing over and over again in searing heat.
- Willingness to work long hours for little or no financial reward essential.
- Would suit someone with extremely limited career options.

Cotton Clothes

Cotton has been made into clothes for thousands of years, since someone somewhere discovered that the fluffy, candyfloss-like stuff produced by cotton plants could be woven into cloth. The plants need a warm climate, and today they're found in China, India, Africa, Australia, South America and the southern United States. To make lots of clothes cheaply and quickly, huge fields of cotton plants are grown – and someone has to pick it.

Hot, Boring and Badly Paid

Picking cotton is boring and repetitive and it's carried out in very hot sun with absolutely no shade (the cotton harvest is in the summertime, and places where cotton is grown tend to have hot summers). The dried bristles on the plants can cut the pickers' fingers and wrists.

Maybe all this wouldn't be so bad if the hours and the money were OK . . . but they aren't.

Poor people have worked as cotton pickers for centuries from dawn to dusk and for very little money. On the plantations of the southern United States, slaves were used to picking cotton (so they didn't get anything at all for their hard work), until slavery was abolished in the nineteenth century.

After that, the people were free but still had to work incredibly hard to survive, because they were paid so little. Most cotton pickers were (and still are) paid by the amount of cotton they pick, not by the number of hours they work, which is a good deal for the owner of the cotton field but not so good for the pickers.

Cotton Picking Today

Today huge machines like combine harvesters pick cotton, though in some parts of the world it's still picked by hand – by children in some cases – and it was picked by hand everywhere until the middle of the twentieth century.

WHIPPING BOY

WANTED: Whipping Boy

DUTIES: Being punished for the royal prince's misdemeanours.

SALARY: None. But you probably won't need one, since your family's absolutely minted anyway.

KEY SKILLS AND ATTRIBUTES:
- Must be a friend of the royal prince.
- High pain threshold a definite advantage.
- Total loyalty to the royal family essential.
- Would suit son of an aristocrat.

To teach badly behaved pupils a lesson, teachers used to hit them. But a royal prince couldn't be whipped, so someone else had to be beaten instead when he did something wrong. Enter the whipping boy...

Whacking in School

Until quite recently it was considered absolutely fine for a teacher to give a pupil a good whack with a big stick if the pupil was misbehaving. In the Middle Ages, it was considered a necessary part of the job – you couldn't have a teacher who didn't beat the children he was teaching – after all, there had to be *some* discipline.

At one school in Cambridge during the Middle Ages, teachers would start the school year by showing off their whacking skills on one of the innocent local children (who wouldn't have been anywhere near rich enough to go to the school and receive beatings for doing something wrong).

Royal Whacking

An English royal prince, however, couldn't be beaten, because according to ideas about royalty at the time, God would have been very cross about it. The answer to this problem was the royal whipping boy, who stood in for the royal prince and had his bottom whacked with a cane instead of the prince if he'd done something wrong.

The whipping boy would have been the son of a posh friend of the king's, so he was at least rich and well educated, and being so close to the future king would mean he'd end up with an enormous house and he'd probably be made a duke or something similar, if he wasn't one already.

William Murray, Charles I's whipping boy, remained close friends with the king once they'd grown up, and became the Earl of Dysart. Barnaby Fitzpatrick, whipping boy for Henry VIII's son, Edward VI, was the son of a baron.

By the way, there were no whipping girls – that's because education for girls, even royal ones, wasn't considered particularly important.

Grown-Up Whipping Boys

A similar sort of thing continued even once the royals had finished their school days. Henri IV of France sent his representatives, D'Ossat and Du Perron, to the Pope when he'd done something wrong, and they were beaten instead of him. He probably felt really bad about it, though.

Modern Whipping Boys

No one does the job of a whipping boy today – thankfully, things have changed since the 1600s. But we still use the term to mean someone who gets the blame or punishment for something someone else has done.

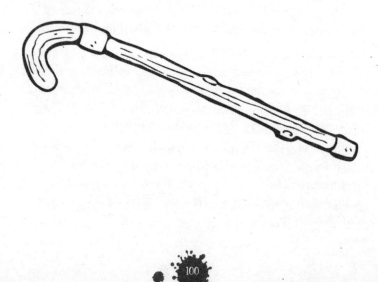

SPIT BOY

WANTED: Spit Boy

DUTIES: Turning a spit to roast meat.

SALARY: £££

KEY SKILLS AND ATTRIBUTES:
- Ability to withstand extreme heat would be an advantage.
- Upper body strength essential.
- Vegetarians need not apply.
- Would suit strong man who isn't easily bored.

You might enjoy a Sunday roast, but maybe you'd be less keen if you had to turn an enormous piece of meat over a fire on a huge metal skewer for hours on end.

Roasting

In the days before gas and electric ovens, people in Europe roasted their meat on a spit. A spit was a long metal spike – you stuck your meat onto it – then lit a fire underneath it. The meat would only be cooked on one side if it wasn't turned, so spits had handles that were operated by men known as spit boys.

They weren't actually children, they were called 'boys' as a sort of insult. They had to be strong to turn a huge spit, and the heavy work had to be done in the fierce heat of the fire. In fact the spit boy would have to be careful not to get roasted himself. There were no toilet breaks, and a working day would start at 4am and could last for serveral hours.

Whole animals were often roasted, and big ones would take a long time to roast, so the spit boy would be hot, exhausted and very, very bored.

Posh Nosh

Most people would eat their meat boiled or dried, which was a good way of making a pig you killed in autumn last the whole winter before fridges were invented. It was only the very rich who would have massive kitchens with great big spits in them turned by servants.

Really rich people liked to eat meat a lot, partly because it tasted nice and partly to show off – so spit boys were in demand. At Hampton Court Palace, where Henry VIII and Elizabeth I lived, the spit boys had to cope with thousands of cows, sheep, deer and pigs every year. They were paid well – six times what a farm labourer would get – but then it *was* a really horrible job.

ANCIENT ROMAN SLAVE

WANTED: Slave

DUTIES: Varied.

SALARY: None at all.

KEY SKILLS AND ATTRIBUTES:
- No experience necessary.
- Work of some kind will be found for you, even if you're half dead.
- Suitable for adults and children of all ages.

Just about the worst thing that can happen to you is having your freedom taken away. At least a quarter of the population of ancient Rome were slaves – people who were owned by others and had no choice about where they lived, the work they did or how they were treated.

Conquering Romans

The ancient Romans were famous for conquering – they did loads of it, and were very good at it. The prisoners taken from the enemy army were often forced to become slaves, and sometimes the Roman Army rounded up the civilians of an area they'd just conquered and made them slaves too.

For example, during Julius Caesar's conquest of Gaul (modern-day France, plus a few other bits of neighbouring countries), he defeated the Veneti tribe in battle and sold the whole lot of them into slavery – around 60,000 men, women and children. Any children who were born to a slave mother became slaves themselves.

As well as unfortunate conquered people, abandoned children could be made into slaves, people who became badly in debt could be made into slaves, and sometimes very poor families might even sell a child into slavery.

Lots of Jobs

Ancient Rome relied on slaves to keep its economy going. Some slaves worked as household servants, doing a variety of different jobs: some were cooks (rich people were keen on finding slaves who were good cooks, so they were very expensive to buy), others might be cleaners or maids, and some might be tutors for the children.

Slaves also worked as shop assistants, accountants and clerks – just the same sorts of jobs you find in cities and towns today, except the people doing them had a lot less choice about what they did. Many slaves worked on latifundia, which were huge farms all over the Roman

Empire owned by the rich. These slaves would have had a hard life doing backbreaking work. Life was worse still for the slaves who mined the metals – gold, silver, copper and tin – used all over the empire. Lots of the slaves working in mines were ex-criminals.

Slave Masters

The people who owned slaves could more or less do what they liked with them. Some slaves might be treated well, almost as family members, while others were beaten and abused – masters could beat their slaves and lots did (though the law changed and it became illegal to physically injure slaves – no one knows how many masters took any notice of it).

A Roman festival called Saturnalia involved jokes, tricks and general mayhem, and sometimes masters swapped places with their slaves – just for the day, of course, but it shows that some slaves and their masters must have got on all right.

Freedom!

The light at the end of the tunnel for a Roman slave was the hope of one day becoming free. Slaves could be freed by their masters, or they could buy their own freedom if they were lucky enough to have found a source of income.

There were lots of freedmen and women in the Roman Empire, and they could become wealthy (and employ slaves of their own). Although being a slave must be the world's worst job, at least ancient Roman slaves weren't seen as a separate, lower class from everyone else.

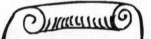

To find out more about slavery, see the Cotton Picker section on page 94.

How to Avoid the World's Worst Jobs

Now you know which jobs to try and avoid: generally, anything that entails poison, sewage, explosives or physical pain. Luckily, you'll almost certainly have a choice about your career, and a lot of jobs which were very dangerous in the past are now much safer.

Working to Live

Most horrible jobs were (or still are) done by people who had no choice – if you were born the son or daughter of a woad dyer, you'd probably end up dying woad (and smelling bad and turning blue) whether you liked the idea or not. If you were an orphan with no money in Victorian England, you might well find yourself stuck up a narrow chimney covered in soot and cuts and bruises.

Millions of people had no education at all, and never found out whether or not they had a talent for running a business, or hairdressing, or scientific research. They just had to get on with whatever was available to them in order to pay for food and somewhere to live.

Learning to Work

In the past, a lot of the world's worst jobs were done by children and in some countries, they still are. Luckily, in most countries today you'll probably have the opportunity to go to school and get an education until you're at least 16, which should help you to have more choice about what you do for a career. Now that is a very good thing . . . unless you go to the world's worst school!

Glossary

abscess
Cavity or hole filled with infected pus

apprentice
Beginner learning an art or trade from someone more experienced

attribute
Quality or personality trait

bile (black or yellow)
Bitter liquid made by the gall bladder used to aid digestion

blood-letting
Draining blood from a person on purpose

cess pit
Large hole in the ground to collect toilet waste

cholera
Disease causing diarrhoea and vomiting which was often fatal

discharge
Liquid, such as pus, which leaks out of a wound

disembowel
Remove someone's intestines and other internal organs

dysentery
Disease causing diarrhoea which is often fatal

fertiliser
Material added to soil to increase its ability to grow crops

firedamp
Highly flammable mixture of methane and other gases often found in coal mines

flammable
Something which can easily catch fire or explode

flue
Shaft used to carry smoke from a chimney to the chimney pot on the roof

guillemot
Black and white seabird

Hoplomachus
Gladiator dressed to look like a Greek hoplite soldier, with heavy armour and a helmet, a round shield, a spear and a sword

humours
Four fluids of the body (blood, phlegm, yellow bile and black bile) which doctors once believed controlled a person's physical and mental health

hydrogen sulphide
Poisonous, flammable gas which smells of rotten eggs

hypothermia
Dangerously low body temperature caused by exposure to extreme cold

immune system
System in the body that detects and fights infections and disease

industrial revolution
Period of time between 1750 to 1850 when huge advances in technology changed the way people lived and worked

infection
Disease which enters the body as bacteria or a virus

Kevlar
Synthetic material that can be woven into fabric and is incredibly strong

leech
Type of freshwater worm that sucks blood

leptospirosis (Weil's disease)
Disease caught from contact with infected water, which if left untreated can sometimes be fatal

mercury nitrate
Chemical used to turn fur into felt for making hats, which is extremely toxic

methane
Colourless, odourless gas produced by humans and other animals

misdemeanour
Crime or bad deed

Murmillo
Gladiator with the short sword and shield of a Roman soldier and a helmet shaped like a fish

phosphorous necrosis
Deadly disease of the jaw caused by the toxic chemical white phosphorous which was once used in matchmaking

phlegm
Clear slimy discharge produced by the walls of the breathing passages

pitch
Roll or lurch at an angle

radioactive
Substance that emits radiation, which can be toxic in large doses

resin
Sticky, fresh smelling liquid produced by plants and trees

Retiarius
Gladiator armed with a three-pronged spear (a trident) and a net

rigid hierarchy
Formal system for organising people into different levels of importance

robust
Strong or powerful

Sagittarius
Gladiator armed with a bow and arrow

salmonella
Type of bacteria which can cause serious food poisoning

Saturnalia
Ancient Roman festival where slaves and their owners swapped roles for the day

specialism
Area in which a person has expert knowledge

squeamish
Easily sickened by the sight of blood, gore or injuries

stool
Poo

synthetic
Man-made

tanner
Person who makes leather from animal skins

tosher
Person who searches for valuables in the sewers for a living

typhoid
Serious and often fatal bacterial infection of the gut

typhus
Disease that causes a fever and severe headaches, which is spread by ticks and fleas

ventilation
Circulation of fresh air

VIP
Very important person

white phosphorous
Toxic chemical used in matchmaking that caused the often fatal disease phosphorous necrosis

woad
Plant which was used to make blue dye

INDEX

Further Information

Books

Poo! A History of the World from the Bottom Up
by Sarah Albee (A & C Black, 2012)

The Horrible History of the World
by Terry Deary and Martin Brown (Scholastic, 2007)

The Worst Children's Jobs In History
by Tony Robinson (Macmillan Children's Books, 2005)

Tough Jobs: Gladiator; Tough Jobs: Knight; Tough Jobs: Pirate
by Helen Gratehead (all three books published by A & C Black, 2008)

Websites

Florence Nightingale
www.bbc.co.uk/schools/primaryhistory/famouspeople/florence_nightingale
Find out why Florence nightingale was famous and why hospitals in
the Crimea were so horrible.

Children at Work in America from 1908-1912
www.eyewitnesstohistory.com/hnintro.htm
See photos and read about young workers in America.

Victorian Children at Work
www.bbc.co.uk/schools/primaryhistory/victorian_britain/victorian_
children_at_work
Find out why so many Victorian children had to work and what they did.

Documentaries

Worst Jobs in History
www.channel4.com/programmes/the-worst-jobs-in-history
This five-part television series produced by Channel 4 sees Tony Robinson explore
some of the worst jobs in history.

About the Author

Tracey Turner has written more than 30 books for children on a variety of subjects,
from rude words to the entire history of the universe. Her books include the best-
selling *101 Things You Need to Know*, *Hard Nuts of History*, *Dreadful Fates*, and
many, many more. She lives in Bath with Tom and their son Toby.